SNAKE-A -PHOBIA

GRACE NORWICH

SCHOLASTIC INC.
NEW YORK • TORONTO • LONDON • AUCKLAND
SYDNEY • MEXICO CITY • NEW DELHI • HONG KONG

Photo credits: front cover left & page 1 left: Audrey Snider-Bell/Shutterstock; front cover right & page 1 right: Imagemore Co., Ltd./Getty Images; page 2 background & pages 40–41 background: Eric Isselée/iStockphoto; page 3 & back cover top right: Eric Isselée/Shutterstock; pages 4–5: pokosuke/iStockphoto; page 4 top inset: Bob Elsdale/Getty Images; page 4 bottom inset: Theo Allofs/Getty Images; page 5 inset: Robert Likar/Shutterstock; pages 6–7 background, pages 14–15 background, & pages 22–23 background: Tania A/Shutterstock; pages 6–7: ANP/Shutterstock; page 6 top inset: Lee Pettet (RF)/Getty Images; page 6 bottom inset: Vicky Kasala Productions (RF)/Getty Images; page 7 & back cover top left: iStockphoto; page 7 inset: www.CartoonStock.com; pages 8–9 background & page 16 background: Pakmo/Shutterstock; pages 8–9: darren pearson/Getty Images; page 9 inset: Tom Walker/Getty Images; pages 10–11 background, pages 18–19 background, & page 43 background: Siede Preis/Getty Images; page 10: Peter Ginter/Getty Images; page 11 left: Claus Meyer/Getty Images; page 11 right: John Foxx/Getty Images; pages 12–13 background & pages 20–21 background: Siede Preis/Getty Images; page 12: Anthony Bannister/Getty Images; page 13 & back cover bottom: Kevin Horan/Getty Images; page 13 inset: Mark Kostich/Getty Images; page 14: Martin Harvey (RF)/Getty Images; page 15 left: Pat Gaines (RF)/Getty Images; page 15 right: Jim Merli/Getty Images; page 16: Volodymyr Pylypchuk/Shutterstock; page 17: defpicture/Shutterstock; page 17 inset: Theo Allofs/Getty Images; pages 18–19: M. Rosley Omar/Shutterstock; page 18 left inset: James Bowyer/iStockphoto; page 18 right inset: Jeffrey Coolidge (RF)/Getty Images; page 19 left inset: Jim Merli/Getty Images; page 19 right inset: Joyce Mar/Shutterstock; pages 20–21: nicola vernizzi/iStockphoto; page 20 inset: David Maitl/Getty Images; page 21 inset: worldswildlifewonders/Shutterstock; pages 22–23: Ronnie Wilson/iStockphoto; page 23 left inset: Tom Ulrich/Getty Images; page 23 right inset: erllre74/Shutterstock; pages 24–25: Jim Larkin/iStockphoto; page 24 top inset: Theo Allofs/Getty Images; page 24 bottom inset: Michael & Patricia Fogden/Minden Pictures/Getty Images; page 25: Mark Kostich/iStockphoto; page 25 top inset: Michael Blann/Getty Images; page 25 bottom inset: Ryan McVay/Getty Images; pages 26–27 background: Don Farrall/Getty Images; page 26: Albert Lleal/Getty Images; page 27: Joel Sartore/Getty Images; page 27 inset: Nigel Dennis/Gallo Images/Getty Images; pages 28–29 background: Devon Stephens/iStockphoto; pages 28–29: Hannamariah/Shutterstock; page 29 left inset: Claus Meyer/Minden Pictures; page 29 right inset: Timothy Laman/Getty Images; pages 30–31 background: Javarman/Shutterstock; pages 30–31: Phil Scher/Getty Images; page 31 left inset: George Grall/Getty Images; page 31 right inset: Peter Chadwick/Getty Images; pages 32–33 background: ANP/Shutterstock; pages 32–33: Jeremy Woodhouse (RF)/Getty Images; page 33 top inset: James R. D. Scott/Shutterstock; page 33 bottom inset: Ryan M. Bolton/Shutterstock; pages 34–35: Willem Tims/Shutterstock; page 34 inset: gabor2100/Shutterstock; page 35 inset: Arie v.d. Wolde/Shutterstock; pages 36–37 background: Thumb/Shutterstock; page 36 top inset: Jake Holmes/iStockphoto; page 36 center inset: Ryan M. Bolton/Shutterstock; page 36 bottom inset: Jason Mintzer/Shutterstock; page 37 top inset: Bruce MacQueen/Shutterstock; page 37 center inset: Jason Patrick Ross/Shutterstock; page 37 bottom inset: Mark Kostich/iStockphoto; pages 38–39: Jason Mintzer/Shutterstock; page 39 top inset: Roy Toft/Getty Images; page 39 center inset: Maria Dryfhout/iStockphoto; page 39 bottom inset: Rusty Dodson/Shutterstock; page 40: Federico Veronesi/Getty Images; page 40 inset: Dave Hamman/Getty Images; page 41 top inset: LiteChoices/Shutterstock; page 41 center inset: Brian Klutch/Getty Images; page 41 bottom inset: Don Klumpp/Getty Images; pages 42–43: Arie v.d. Wolde/Shutterstock; page 43: AZPworldwide/Shutterstock; page 43 inset: Joel Sartore/Getty Images; pages 44–45 background: Suto Norbert Zsolt; page 44 top inset: Ingo Arndt/Minden Pictures; page 44 bottom inset: Shannon Plummer/Peter Arnold, Inc.; page 45 top inset: Michael Richards/John Downer/Nature Picture Library; page 45 center inset: Ch'ien Lee/Minden Pictures; page 45 bottom inset: Claus Meyer/Minden Pictures; pages 46–47: Angelo Giampiccolo/Shutterstock; page 47 top: Arie v.d. Wolde/Shutterstock; page 47 bottom: Thomas Marent/Minden Pictures/Getty Images; page 48 background: Siede Preis/Getty Images; back cover background: James Bowyer/iStockphoto

ISBN 978-0-545-27332-9

10 9 8 7 6 5 4 3 2 1   11 12 13 14 15

Printed in the U.S.A.   40

First printing, January 2011
Design by Kay Petronio

CONTENTS

INTRODUCTION

The forest is quiet. Even the leaves in the trees are still. All of a sudden . . . *hissssssss!!!* A tail slinks behind a nearby tree. What could it be? There it goes again, a slithering beast all covered in scales! It's under a rock now. Two beady eyes peer out from the shadows. The hissing stops, only to be replaced by a terrifying rattle. Just then a head appears. The creature opens its mouth wide, revealing a set of pointy fangs. That can only mean one thing:

It must be . . . it's a . . . SNAKE!!!

There's no doubt about it, snakes seem like the scariest creatures on the planet. If you've ever seen one slither across your path in the woods or grass, you know what we mean. Yeeks! But do snakes deserve their fearsome reputation? Not really.

Not all snakes are harmless. In this book, you'll meet a few that you *definitely* want to avoid (unless they're behind glass at the zoo!). But for the most part, snakes are pretty innocent. So why are so many people terrified of them? The answer has to do with a curious little word: *PHOBIA*.

OPHIDIO-WHAT?

pho·bia (noun)
"An exaggerated, usually inexplicable and illogical fear of a particular object, class of objects, or situation."

—*Merriam-Webster's Online Dictionary*

In other words, having a phobia means that there is something you're very afraid of, even though there's really no need to be. A lot of people suffer from snake phobia in a big way. Doctors even have a special name for it: *ophidiophobia.*

Check out this list of other common phobias:

Acrophobia: the fear of heights

Arachnophobia: the fear of spiders

Astraphobia: the fear of thunder and lightning

Cynophobia: the fear of dogs

Pteromerhanophobia: the fear of flying

So how do you know if you have ophidiophobia? For one thing, you definitely want to run away anytime you come near one of these slithering creatures. If you're a true snake-phobe, even a picture of a snake in a book or on television is enough to give you the willies. You'll probably feel your heart pounding faster in your chest. You might also break out into a cold sweat and have trouble catching your breath. These are all sure signs of snake phobia. The good news is, you can probably get over your fear of snakes.

It doesn't matter that we're not venomous: Most people stay well clear of us anyway...

www.CartoonStock.com

CONQUERING YOUR FEAR

Step one is figuring out why you're so afraid of snakes. There might be one reason for your snake phobia, or there might be a few reasons. Either way, the next step in conquering your fear of snakes is learning more about them. Stuff always seems less scary when you understand it really well. For example, someone with pteromerhanophobia (remember, that's the fear of flying) might be able to get over that phobia by studying how planes work.

SNAKES 101

Let's learn more about what makes a snake a snake. Snakes are reptiles. All reptiles are cold-blooded, which means that their body temperature is the same as the temperature of the surrounding air. They keep warm by lying in the sun or on a hot rock. Lizards, turtles, and alligators are other members of the reptile family.

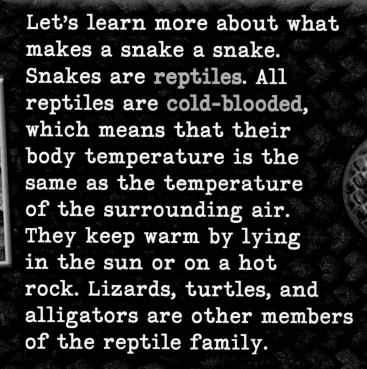

FEAR-O-METER: HIGH

low   medium   high

Here are the different parts of the snake. Next to each body part you'll find a Fear-o-meter. This will tell you how scary this part is to other snake-phobes.

FANGS

10

A lot of people with snake phobia are very afraid of getting bitten by a snake. For this reason, fangs are one of a snake's most terrifying features. Fangs are found only on poisonous snakes. When one of these snakes bites its victim, poisonous venom flows out of special glands in the snake's head. The venom then passes through its hollow fangs and into the victim's body.

FRIGHT BITE

Doctors use snake venom to make medicines that help save people who are bitten by poisonous snakes.

MOUTH

The bones of a snake's upper and lower jaws can move apart. As a result, snakes can open their mouths very wide. This allows snakes to eat animals that are much larger than they are. Snakes also have teeth, but they don't use them to chew the way humans do. Instead, a snake's teeth are used to hold a victim in place, kind of like a trap.

FRIGHT BITE

A snake can eat animals that are three times larger than the **diameter** of its head.

TONGUE

A human uses its nose to smell. But a snake uses its tongue. This is why a snake's tongue has a fork in it. The shape helps the snake sniff out odors from different spots at once. It's also why a snake flicks its tongue a lot. The movement of the tongue helps pick up smells in the air. Snake-phobes often think that the flicking tongue makes the hissing sound and is a sign that a snake is about to attack. But really, a snake hisses for self-defense, and the flicking is just a way for the snake to smell better.

14

FRIGHT BITE

Some snakes play dead when a **predator** attacks. The hognose snake goes limp and lets its tongue dangle from its mouth.

BODY

A snake's body is made up of one long backbone with many pairs of ribs coming off it. The ribs are all wrapped in muscle. Snakes use their bodies to move in different ways. Some wriggle along the ground in curves. Some move in a straight line, or up and down like accordions. And some move in sudden sideways motions, which is called sidewinding. This last form of motion is maybe the most frightening, since it happens so quickly.

FRIGHT BITE

There's one other scary thing about a snake's body. Some snakes use their bodies to suffocate their **prey** by wrapping around it and not letting go. Each time the victim takes a breath, the snake squeezes tighter. This is called **constricting**— and, yes, it's pretty terrifying!

SCALES

FEAR-O-METER: MEDIUM

low   medium   high

18

Like all members of the reptile family, snakes are covered in scales. The scales are thick and hard, especially the ones along the snake's belly. These tough scales protect the snake as it slithers on the ground. Scales are often brightly colored and arranged in interesting patterns. Snakes with colorful scales are sometimes poisonous. But some non-poisonous snakes have bright colors that are designed to trick predators into thinking they're more dangerous than they really are.

FRIGHT BITE

Snakes never stop growing. They have to shed their skin at least twice a year, and more when they're young. This process is called **molting**. A snake's skin comes off in one complete piece, including the part over the eyes. For some snake-phobes, molting is the creepiest thing of all about snakes.

19

EYES

low   medium   high

20

Unlike people and other animals, snakes don't have eyelids. Instead, each eye is covered with a hard shell called a brille that is part of the snake's skin. Because the brille is clear, it looks like a snake's eyes are always open—and like it's staring right at you! A lot of snake-phobes are seriously freaked out by this. But the truth is, snakes can't see very well. So they're definitely not sizing you up as a tasty treat.

FRIGHT BITE

As cold-blooded creatures, all snakes are sensitive to temperature changes. But thanks to special sensory pits in its head, the pit viper can detect changes as little as less than half of a degree. That ability allows this snake to strike at **warm-blooded** prey in total darkness.

21

TAIL

low medium high

22

The tail on most snakes is just the end of the body. Nothing scary about that. But some snakes have a rattle on their tails that they use to make an eerie buzzing sound. This rattle is actually a collection of rings that form each time the snake sheds its skin. Some people believe that you can tell how old a snake is by how many rings it has. But this isn't true, since pieces of the rattle sometimes break off.

FRIGHT BITE

Snakes are a farmer's best friends. That's because they eat rodents and other small animals that feed on crops.

SNAKES BY THE NUMBERS

2,900 — approximate number of snake species

375 — number of species of venomous snakes

44 — diameter (in inches) of the thickest snake

40 — age (in years) of the oldest snake

33 — length (in feet) of the longest measured snake

4 — approximate length (in inches) of the shortest measured snake

FRIGHT BITE

Snakes can go many months between meals. Pythons and other large snakes can survive for an entire year without eating.

WHERE TO FIND SNAKES

(and where to not find them!)

Snakes can be found in many types of habitats. They like to live in places where the weather is warm. Snakes can be found in colder places, but not as often. And you rarely see snakes in cities, unless it's inside a zoo or pet shop. Here are some of a snake's favorite hangouts.

DESERT

More than one-fifth of Earth's surface is covered in desert. That makes this dry spot one of the snake's largest slithering grounds. Snakes don't sweat, so they're able to survive without losing too much fluid under the hot, baking sun. It also helps that they can go years without drinking water! They feed on rodents and other small creatures that live in the desert.

COMMON DESERT SNAKES

horned viper

western diamondback rattlesnake

TROPICAL RAIN FOREST

This habitat is found around the equator, at the middle of the earth. Rain forests are hot, humid, and often rainy. This results in a lot of thick vegetation, including trees. Many tropical snakes make their homes in these trees. Some of the largest, most dangerous snakes live in the tropics. So if you're a snake-phobe, the rain forest might not be the place for you!

COMMON RAIN FOREST SNAKES

anaconda

reticulated
python

GRASSLANDS

Many snakes like to hang out in these grassy habitats, which also cover a large part of the planet. These areas are home to many other animals that snakes like to eat, including field mice and birds. But snakes have to be careful in grasslands, since a lot of their enemies live there as well, such as hawks, foxes, and badgers.

COMMON GRASSLAND SNAKES

eastern hognose

puff adder

WATER

You probably think of fish as living in water. But plenty of snakes make their homes there, too. Some like freshwater rivers, lakes, and ponds. Others prefer saltwater oceans and seas. Water snakes still need air to breathe, but many can stay underwater for hours without coming up for air.

COMMON WATER SNAKES

banded
sea snake

mud snake

SNAKE-FREE ZONES

Antarctica is the only continent on Earth that doesn't have any snakes. That's because snakes can't survive where the ground is permanently frozen. Unfortunately, most people find the freezing temperatures in Antarctica unbearable as well. But a few island nations around the world are also pretty much snake-free. These include Ireland, Iceland, and New Zealand. So if all other cures fail for snake-phobes, they can always move to one of these places!

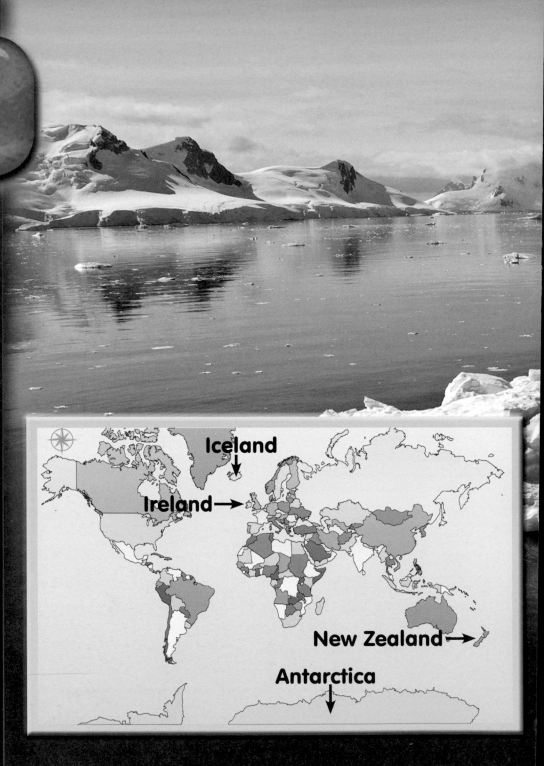

Iceland

Ireland→

New Zealand→

Antarctica

NO SNAKES ALLOWED!

THE UNITED SNAKES OF AMERICA

The United States is definitely home to a lot of snakes. More than 125 different species are found in North America. While some of these are poisonous, the vast majority are completely harmless to people. Here are a few you might encounter if you spend enough time out in nature:

southern copperhead coiled snake

blunthead tree snake

mountain kingsnake

garter snakes

gray rat snake

water moccasin snake

GARTER SNAKE: You're most likely to encounter this snake, which lives happily in forests, in fields, and even around humans. But don't worry—it's completely harmless.

RAT SNAKE: This snake gets its name from the fact that it likes to eat rats and other rodents. Though harmless, it sometimes has the coloring of a poisonous cobra.

WATER SNAKE: Different species of this snake are found in rivers, lakes, and ponds all over the country.

HOW TO PROTECT YOURSELF

Since snakes are common in North America, it pays to be careful. Here are three ways to stay protected:

1 When you're out walking in the woods, wear long pants to protect your legs and heavy shoes that will protect your feet.

2 Never stick your hands or feet inside places that could serve

as hiding spots for snakes. That includes trash piles and high weeds or grasses.

3 If you come across a snake, avoid it. Never try to handle a snake, even if you're sure it's not poisonous. Bites from non-poisonous snakes can still be painful. If you ever do get bitten, call for help immediately and try to remember what the snake looked like. This will help doctors determine the best course of treatment.

WHAT MAKES SNAKES SCARED

Snakes have a lot of enemies in nature. One of the most famous snake hunters is the mongoose, which will even attack poisonous snakes. Other animals that like to eat snakes are lions, leopards, raccoons, foxes, and certain monkeys. Snakes also have to be on the lookout for birds of prey, including hawks, eagles, and falcons.

But humans may be the biggest enemy of all for snakes. Many people try to capture snakes to sell as pets. Others hunt them for their skins, which can be used to make shoes, handbags, belts, and more. Last but not least, snake habitats are often destroyed to make room for roads and buildings. There are more than fifty types of snake on the endangered species list around the world. That means that these snakes are in danger of being wiped out from existence.

SNAKE TEST #1

1. Which of the following is the biggest threat to snakes?

A) Eagles
B) Mongooses
C) Humans
D) Other snakes

2. About how many different types of snakes are there?

A) 200
B) 700
C) 2,900
D) 30,000

3. Where would you be most likely to see a snake?

A) United States
B) Antarctica
C) Ireland
D) New Zealand

4. Which of these North American snakes is the most common?

A) Rattlesnake
B) Garter snake
C) Water snake
D) Rat snake

5. What is the best way to avoid getting bitten by a snake?

A) Wear long pants
B) Don't walk through high weeds
C) Steer clear of dark holes
D) All of the above

THE WORLD'S MOST DANGEROUS SNAKES

Here are five snakes that you definitely don't want to get anywhere near:

GREEN ANACONDA
Where it lives:
South America
Why it's so scary:
The green anaconda is one of the world's largest snakes. It often waits underwater for animals to come and drink, and then attacks. It can eat a whole deer!

FIERCE SNAKE
Where it lives:
Australia
Why it's so scary:
The fierce snake didn't get its name for nothing. It's actually considered the most poisonous land snake in the world. Fortunately, this snake lives deep in the Australian desert, so you don't have to worry about running into one.

green anaconda

fierce snake

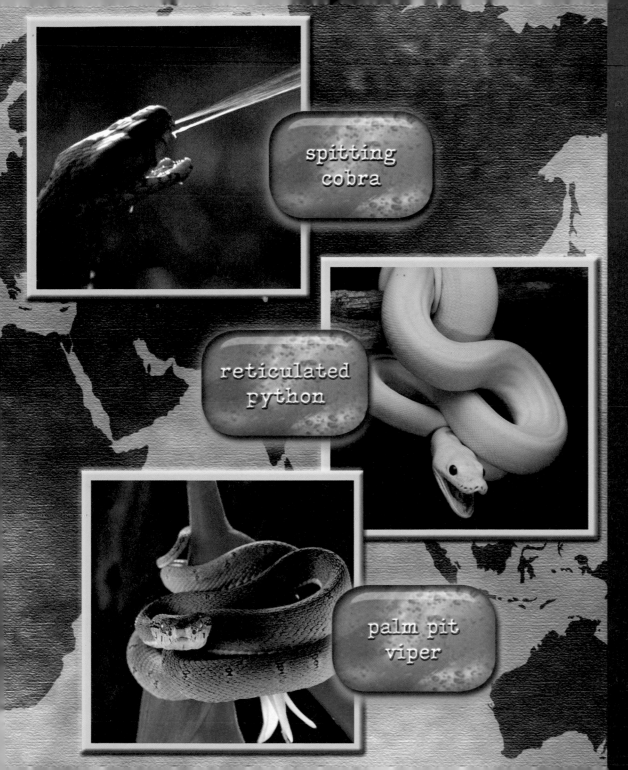

spitting
cobra

reticulated
python

palm pit
viper

SPITTING COBRA
Where it lives:
Asia and Africa
Why it's so scary:
This snake can spray its poisonous venom up to eight feet in the air. It will sometimes aim for its enemy's eyes.

RETICULATED PYTHON
Where it lives: Southeast Asia
Why it's so scary:
It's the longest of all snakes, growing as long as a school bus in some cases. It squeezes its prey to death by wrapping around it.

PALM PIT VIPER
Where it lives:
Central and South America
Why it's so scary:
This poisonous snake lives in small palm trees and bushes that are about as tall as a grown person. As a result, when it attacks people, it usually strikes them in the face.

SNAKE TEST #2

1. Snakes are scared of people.

TRUE!

Even the most dangerous snakes in the world will do whatever they can to avoid human contact. It's only when a snake is feeling threatened or surprised that it will try to bite a person. But the snake will always try to escape or frighten off the person first.

2. Snakes are slimy.

FALSE!

A lot of people are afraid of snakes because they think their skin is slimy. But, in fact, a snake's skin is dry and rough. It has to be in order to protect the snake's body and keep it from drying out.

3. Snakes smell with their mouths.

TRUE!

A snake sticks out its tongue to bring smells from the air into its mouth. A special organ at the roof of its mouth called the Jacobson's organ identifies the different smells.

4. Some snakes crush their prey to death.

FALSE!

A few snakes kill their victims by wrapping their bodies around them and squeezing tight. But they don't actually crush their victims to death. Instead, they keep squeezing until their victims can no longer breathe.

5. All brightly colored snakes are poisonous.

FALSE!

It's true that snakes with bright, colorful scales are often venomous. But some snakes mimic these colorful patterns to trick other animals into thinking they're venomous. Still, if you ever come across a snake that's brightly colored, don't take any chances.

GLOSSARY

Brille: the clear cap that protects each of a snake's eyes

Cold-blooded: having a body temperature that changes with the temperature of the environment

Constrict: to compress or squeeze

Diameter: the width of a circular object

Endangered: being in danger of becoming extinct

Habitat: the environment where an animal lives

Humid: containing a lot of moisture (like the air can be)

Molt: to shed an outer layer of skin

Predator: an animal that hunts and eats other animals to survive

Prey: an animal that is hunted by other animals for food

Reptile: a cold-blooded animal, usually covered with scales, that crawls on short legs or moves on its belly

Sidewind: to move by rolling the body in a sideways, looping motion

Species: one of the groups into which animals and plants are divided

Vegetation: plant life

Venom: a poisonous liquid that some snakes produce

Warm-blooded: having a body temperature that stays the same, no matter the temperature outside